LOVE YOUR BODY

by Jessica Sanders
illustrated by Carol Rossetti

FIVE MILE

For Sophie,

your legacy lives on in our hearts
and through our actions.

J.S.

FIVE MILE

Five Mile, the publishing division of Regency Media
www.fivemile.com.au

This paperback edition first published 2022

Written by Jessica Sanders
Illustrations by Carol Rossetti

Visit: www.re-shape.info

Jessica Sanders asserts her right to be identified as the author of this work.
Carol Rossetti asserts her right to be identified as the illustrator of this work.
Designed by Stephanie Spartels, Studio Spartels.

ISBN 978-1-92267-708-2 (pbk)

Printed in China 5 4 3 2 1

A catalogue record for this book is available from the National Library of Australia

NOTE TO THE READER

To the girls,

It is my hope that this book will comfort you, guide you and empower you. I want you to know that you are extraordinary exactly as you are. Once you know this to be true nothing will be able to hold you back – you and your incredible body will be able to do anything, so dream big.

Your friend,
Jess

AUTHOR'S NOTE

This book has been written for girls and those who identify as a girl. However, the language I have used is not gendered and the overarching message is universal. Negative body image can affect anyone, regardless of gender, race or sexual orientation. This book draws on my postgraduate studies in gender and social work as well as my own experiences as a girl and young woman struggling with society's unrealistic expectations of 'beauty'. The messages in this book have also been influenced by a body functionality approach, feminist theory and the body positive movement.

Love Your Body has been created to be understood by a range of readers. Children younger than the recommended reading age of 8+ should be able to navigate the book with the support of a parent, carer or teacher.
Even if a child is not able to understand all of the language, they should understand the visual messages. The illustrations send a strong, clear message and it is important that young girls be exposed to this message as early as possible.

Your body is **unique.**

No one has a body quite like yours and that's amazing!

Every body is **different**
and EVERY body is a good body.

Your body is **always changing** and you will notice some of the **biggest changes** when you go through puberty*.

*Puberty is a time when your body changes and grows on the inside and outside to look more like an adult's body.

Going through puberty can feel like a **weird time**. Your body will change on the **inside** and the **outside**. Your body will become bigger and it will take up more space, and **that's okay!**

Bodies come in all different **forms** and **abilities**. All these bodies are different and all these bodies are good bodies.

There is no one **size**, **ability** or **colour** that is perfect. What makes you different makes you, you – and you are **amazing!**

It's important to accept and love yourself exactly as you are. Do not wait until tomorrow, start right now.

They can do so many **incredible** things.

Bodies are not just to be looked at and admired – our bodies are so **much more than that.**

If you are ever finding it hard to love your body, try writing a list of all the great things that your body helps you to do.

Here are some examples.

I love that my ears can hear music and that my body can dance to the sound.

I love that my body is strong enough to pick up my little brother and give him a big cuddle.

I love that my eyes can see
my favourite TV show and
read my favourite book.
I love that my
hands help me to create
beautiful things.
I love that my nose
can smell the saltiness of
the sea and the flowers
in the garden.

If that list isn't working, here is another list of helpful things you can do when you're feeling a little down. Taking time to look after your mind and body is called 'self-care'. Self-care is a great way of showing kindness to yourself and it's a skill you can use throughout your whole life.

1

Stand in front of the mirror and say, "MY BODY IS STRONG. MY BODY CAN DO AMAZING THINGS. MY BODY IS MY OWN."

2

Go outside and connect with nature. Find a nice tree to sit under, or lie on some grass and feel the blades of grass on your skin.

3

Write down three things you are truly grateful for.

4

Put on a crazy and colourful outfit and strut around acting confident until you actually start feeling that way!

5

Put on your favourite tunes REALLY LOUD and dance crazily just for you! You will find a smile creeping onto your face. You won't be able to stop it.

6

Help a friend or family member. It can be a relief to get out of your own head and help others. It will make you feel really good to do something for someone else.

7

Learn how to knit, crochet, cross-stitch or draw mandalas. It's really calming to use your hands and concentrate on one thing.

8

Do some slow stretching in a quiet place; this will help you feel more at home in your body. If you want to, you could try doing some yoga. There are lots of free videos online to help you get started.

9

Try taking photos of things around your house. Looking at life through a camera lens can help you see things differently, and it's a great way to be creative.

10

Search for positive quotes until you find one that has meaning for you. Print it out or write it down, and keep it with you. Look at it when you're feeling down.

If you ever try some of these things and they aren't making you feel better, then it's very important you seek help from a trusted adult or from one of the organisations listed in the back of this book.

Everyone needs to ask for help sometimes – you are **not alone.**

Your body really is quite incredible, and if you listen you can hear it speaking to you. Your body will tell you what it needs by sending signals – it's really smart like that! Your body will let you know when you need to eat, and it will let you know when you need to rest.

Listening to your body and giving it what it needs is another way that you can practise self-care.

Sometimes your body might not be able to do the things you want it to do. And sometimes it might feel like your body is working against you, instead of with you.

When you feel this way, remember that your body is doing the best it can. All bodies are different, and all bodies have different strengths. Find your body's strengths, and love and embrace each one.

You can celebrate your body and show the world who you are by developing your **own style.**

Dress for you and **how you feel.** This might change from day to day, and that's okay! You will feel your happiest when you are just being yourself.

Your body is an **incredible** instrument for you to use.

Use your body to **move,**

laugh,

cry,

hug and feel.

Use your body to live your life in whatever way you choose and know that you are always worthy of love and respect.

Your body is incredible, that is true, but you are so **much more** than your body.

You are **smart**,

curious,

passionate,

fierce,

kind and courageous.

These are just some of the many things that make you, you.

Loving yourself for both what is on the inside and what is on the outside is called 'self-love'.

Self-love can be a journey, full of highs and lows. Self-love is the most important kind of love because the relationship you have with yourself and with your body is the most important relationship you will ever have.

Show your body **love** and **thanks** by practising self-care. Sometimes you will forget and some days it will feel nearly impossible, and that's okay. When this happens just remember to be kind to yourself, speak to yourself like you would your very best friend.

Many of the people around you are also learning how to love their bodies. You can help them by **sharing** the lessons you have learnt in this book, and by showing them the same love and kindness that you would show yourself.

NOW WHAT?

If you notice a little voice in your head saying mean things about your body, remember to be kind to yourself. Tell that little voice, "MY BODY IS STRONG. MY BODY CAN DO AMAZING THINGS. MY BODY IS MY OWN."

Try writing your own self-care list. What activities or thoughts make you feel calm? What makes you happy? Keep your list somewhere close and use it whenever you feel you need it. You can find some self-care suggestions on pages 16 and 17 of this book.

Start a journal. Each day write down how you felt that day. If you had negative thoughts, write down how you dealt with them. If you had positive thoughts, write down how they made you feel. If you enjoy art, why not try drawing, painting or collaging in your journal.

Write down some of the things that you like to do and explain how your body helps you to do them. When you're finding it hard to **love** your body read over your list and you will remember all the reasons why your body is **worth loving**. See pages 14 and 15 of this book for some ideas.

When you hear your friends saying something negative about their bodies, gently remind them of the lessons you have learnt from this book. You can **lift** your friends up by listing all the things you love about their personalities or by **celebrating** the amazing things their bodies can do.

If you're experiencing **negative thoughts**, start a conversation with someone you trust. It's important to share how you are **feeling** with others. Reaching out and seeking help is **incredibly brave**.

EVERYONE NEEDS TO ASK FOR HELP SOMETIMES; YOU ARE NOT ALONE.

Australia

Butterfly Foundation National Helpline – 1800 33 4673
Support for eating disorders and body image concerns.
Online chat: www.thebutterflyfoundation.org.au

Kids Helpline – 1800 55 1800
Contact Kids Helpline at any time, for any reason.
Online chat: https://kidshelpline.com.au/

Headspace – 1800 650 890
Support for young people and their families going through a tough time.
Online chat: https://eheadspace.org.au/

New Zealand

What's Up – 0800 942 8787
A safe place to talk about anything at all.
Online chat: www.whatsup.co.nz

Youth Line – 0800 37 66 33
Support for young people and their families.
Online chat: www.youthline.co.nz

If you live outside Australia and New Zealand, check out the www.re-shape.info website for the support organisations in your country.

RESOURCES

Head to www.re-shape.info to find resources that will support you in learning to love your body.

Younger (7–10)

Printable resources
Support for parents
Mindfulness activities

Older (10–12+)

Social media
Yoga and mindfulness
Puberty

Educator Resources

Lesson plans

My body is strong.

My body can do amazing things.

My body is my own.

Jessica Sanders

Jessica is an author, advocate and social worker from Melbourne, Australia. Growing up, Jessica was always the tallest student in her class, and struggled to accept and love her body. When she was 12, her mother signed her up to play volleyball knowing her height would be celebrated and an advantage. Jessica soon learned that different bodies brought different skills to the team and all these bodies were valued. When Jessica left high school, she travelled solo to many countries and climbed some of the world's highest mountains, always carrying a heavy pack and grateful for her strong body. Over time, and through the ups and downs of life's lessons, Jessica grew to love and celebrate her body. Inspired by her own journey, Jessica wrote *Love Your Body* to educate and empower young girls with the message of self-love. This is a book that Jessica wishes she had growing up. *Love Your Body* is Jessica's gift to young girls everywhere.

Carol Rossetti

Carol is a designer and illustrator from Belo Horizonte, Brazil. Carol is passionate about promoting diversity and women's rights through her art. She has been working as a professional illustrator and designer for seven years and also co-runs a graphic design studio called Café com Chocolate Design. When Carol isn't drawing or painting she loves reading and watching movies.